Little Leif
Loves Local Food

Written by Roberta Jackson and Phillip Joy

Illustrations by Maritza Miari

 FriesenPress

One Printers Way
Altona, MB R0G 0B0
Canada

www.friesenpress.com

ISBN
978-1-03-912646-6 (Hardcover)
978-1-03-912645-9 (Paperback)
978-1-03-912647-3 (eBook)

1. JUVENILE NONFICTION, COOKING & FOOD

Distributed to the trade by The Ingram Book Company

Contents

Foreword

This cookbook is a unique collaboration of artistic talent. It is a celebration of cooking with children and family, and eating locally grown food together. In this book a young girl named Loli shares her joy and anticipation of her favourite foods that arrive with each season. These recipes are connected to Nova Scotia, but the concept of eating locally is universal. It can be done any place you are.

The authors have roots in Nova Scotia, British Columbia and Cuba. They have brought together their love of nutritious recipes made with Nova Scotia's seasonal foods, the fun of cooking as a family, photography, illustration, and the magic that can happen with shared creativity.

Summer

Sticky Summer Pancakes

with Local Strawberry Syrup

3

Little Loli *loves local food.*

Eating puts her in a good mood.

Her Nana makes apple purée,

While she dreams of a summer day.

When strawberry plants grow green shoots

And Loli starts to see new fruits.

In the warm sun and leafy bed,

Loli sees berries turning red.

Soon after they will disappear,

When she gobbles them all up! Cheers!

Sticky Summer Pancakes
with Local Strawberry Syrup

Summer Pancakes

Makes about 8 small pancakes

1/2 cup	125 mL	whole wheat flour
1/2 cup	125 mL	all-purpose flour
1 1/2 tsp	7.5 mL	baking powder
1 cup	250 mL	buttermilk or milk
1/2 tsp	2.5 mL	vanilla extract
2 tbsp	30 mL	vegetable oil
1	1	large egg
1 tbsp	15 mL	sugar (white or brown), honey, or maple syrup

Chef's Tip

Always wash your hands using soap and warm water before preparing food.

Directions:

1. Put the flour and baking powder in a large mixing bowl. Mix together with a fork.

2. In a separate bowl, add the buttermilk, vanilla, vegetable oil, egg, and sugar. Mix with a fork or whisk until the egg is combined.

3. Pour the wet ingredients into the dry ingredients. Stir with a wooden spoon, leaving a few small lumps in the batter. Do not overstir.

4. Preheat a skillet on medium heat for 2–3 minutes. Brush the pan with a bit of oil.

5. Using a ladle, pour the batter into the pan. You can experiment with creating fun shapes.

6. When the edges dry and bubbles appear on top, flip over wit a spatula (about 2 minutes per side). Cook until golden brown.

7. Top with Strawberry Syrup

Strawberry Syrup

3 tbsp	45 mL	sugar (white or brown)
1/4 cup	60 mL	water
2 cups	500 mL	fresh strawberries, chopped or sliced

Directions

1. Place sugar, water and strawberries in a small pot. Bring to a boil over medium heat. Turn the heat down and cook for 10 minutes.

2. Spoon the syrup over pancakes while the berries are warm.

Chef's Tip

For safety, have an adult supervise when using a hot stove and sharp knives.

Fall

Squishy-Squash Fall Soup

with Apples and Lentils

Sweet is summer, but **Loli's** senses are sharp.
She knows when the nights are turning cold and dark.
Fall is calling all the wild children to school.
Days are becoming crisp and five degrees cool.
This time of year her family is busy.
All the activity makes Loli dizzy.
The harvest is hauled from every garden bed.
Nana in the kitchen gets everyone fed.
A pot of squash soup is bubbling away,
Hand-picked from the garden that very same day.
Nothing is quite so delicious and yummy
As fresh muffins and warm soup for your tummy.

Squishy-Squash Fall Soup
with Apples and Lentils

Squishy-Squash Fall Soup

Makes about 8 servings

Chef's Tip

2 tbsp	30 mL	vegetable oil
1	1	medium onion, roughly chopped
1	1	stalk celery, roughly chopped
1	1	medium carrot, roughly chopped
1 tbsp	15 mL	curry powder
1 tsp	5 mL	ginger powder, or
2 tsp	10 mL	fresh ginger
1/4 tsp	1.25 mL	cinnamon
pinch	pinch	nutmeg
½	½	acorn or butternut squash, peeled and chopped into large pieces
1–2	1–2	medium apples (Courtland or Honeycrisp), cut into quarters, with core removed
1/2 cup	125 mL	red lentils, dried
4 cups	1 litre	vegetable stock (low sodium)
1–2 cups	250–500 mL	water (as needed)

Optional:

1/2 cup	125 mL	water, coconut milk, soy milk, or 1% buttermilk
		yogurt and chopped green onions, for topping

Chef's Tip

Try to cut the vegetables into similar-sized pieces so they cook in roughly the same time.

Directions:

1. Using a large soup pot, heat the olive oil over medium heat. Add the onion, celery, carrot and spices. Cook for about 8 minutes, stirring occasionally, until the onions are soft.

2. Add the squash, apples, and lentils to the pot. Pour in the vegetable stock. Bring the soup to a boil, then turn the heat to low and cover

3. Simmer for 30–45 minutes, stirring occasionally. Add 1–2 cups (250–500 mL) water as the soup thickens, to keep the desired consistency.

4. Turn off the heat. Using an immersion blender, blend until smooth

5. If the soup is too thick, add ½ cup (125 mL) water, or, to make it creamy, add coconut milk, soy milk, or buttermilk.

6. Ladle soup into bowls and top with a spoon-ful of yogurt and chopped green onions, or drizzle with coconut milk.

Pumpkin Cornmeal Muffins

Makes 12 small muffins

1 cup	250 mL	yellow cornmeal
1 cup	250 mL	whole wheat flour
1 ½ tsp	7.5 mL	baking powder
½ tsp	2.5 mL	baking soda
¼ tsp	1.25 mL	salt
1	1	large egg
1 cup	250 mL	buttermilk
1 cup	250 mL	pumpkin purée
3 tbsp	45 mL	vegetable oil
2 tbsp	30 mL	maple syrup

Directions

1. Preheat the oven to 400°F (200°C). Grease muffin tins with a little oil or butter.

2. Measure the dry ingredients into a large mixing bowl.

3. In a separate bowl, add the egg, butter-milk, pumpkin purée, vegetable oil, and maple syrup. Mix well with a whisk.

4. Pour the wet ingredients into the dry ingredients and stir gently.

5. Spoon the batter evenly into the muffin cups.

6. Bake for 20–25 minutes.

Winter

Crunchy-Cozy Fish & Rainbow Chips

with Local Root Vegetables

At Loli's window, a cold wind is knocking.
Winter is here, which means layers of stockings,
Scratchy green wool sweaters pulled over her head,
Extra warm blankets at the end of her bed.
Loli's excited because this time of year
Her best uncle Henry will surely appear
At the door, whistling and boots going swish.
One cold morning he'll come with many fish,
The family will greet with hugs and big grins,
It's haddock dinner and they quickly dig in!

Crunchy-Cozy Fish & Rainbow Chips

with Local Root Vegetables

Rainbow Chips

Makes about 4 servings

1 1/2 cups	375 mL	beets, fresh (2 medium)
1 1/2 cups	375 mL	sweet potato (1 medium)
2 cups	500 mL	red- or yellow-skinned pota-toes (2–3 medium)
2 tbsp	30 mL	vegetable oil

Other root vegetables to try: carrots, parsnips, yams, celeriac, or cassava

Chef's Tip

It doesn't matter what the shape is, but try to cut the vegetables into similar-sized pieces so they take the same time to bake.

Directions:

1. Preheat the oven to 400°F (200°C). Wash the root vegetables. Cut into round pieces or sticks.

2. Toss the vegetables with the oil and spread evenly on a baking tray. Bake for 20 minutes. Take the tray out and turn the vegetables so they brown on both sides. Bake for 15–20 minutes more while the fish is prepared.

23

Crunchy-Cozy Fish
Makes about 4 servings

1–1 1/4 lbs	450–600 g	haddock fillets, fresh or frozen
2 tbsp	30 mL	mayonnaise

Crunchy Crust

¼ cup	60 mL	panko bread crumbs
¼ cup	60 mL	sesame seeds
¼ cup	60 mL	Parmesan (optional)
		vegetable oil for frying
1–2 tbsp	15–30 mL	

Chef's Tip

Use a cooking thermometer to test the internal temperature: at least 145°F (65°C) for fish.

Directions

1. While the chips are baking, prepare the haddock. Remove excess moisture from the fillet by patting with paper towel. Lay the fillets on a clean cutting board or large plate.

2. Spoon the mayonnaise into a small bowl. Using a pastry brush, spread mayonnaise in a thin layer on one side.

3. Stir the panko crumbs, sesame seeds, and Parmesan cheese together.

4. Sprinkle the crumb topping onto the mayonnaise side of the fish, covering it thoroughly and pressing it onto the fish. Turn the fish over and repeat with mayonnaise and crumb topping.

5. Preheat a non-stick frying pan on medium heat. Add the oil to the pan. Once the oil is hot, place the prepared haddock in the pan. Fry for about 10 minutes on each side.

6. Arrange the vegetable chips and fish on four plates and serve.

Spring

Bubbling 'n' Bursting Tart
with Fresh Rhubarb

The season has changed again and Loli *takes note.*
There are buds on the trees and first flowers have poked.
Spring has arrived, announced by the green of the grass,
And giant leaves of rhubarb plants growing up fast.
Loli helps Nana tugging stalks from the wet ground
While also playing with slimy snails that she's found.
She'll pucker her lips at the tartness and flavour
But dipped in sweet sugar she knows she will savour.
When Nana and her make their sticky pastry,
Soon the rhubarb will be sweet and oh so tasty.

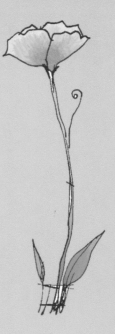

Bubbling 'n' Bursting Tart
with Fresh Rhubarb

Basic Pastry

1 cup	250 mL	flour (whole wheat or all-purpose)
6 tbsp	90 mL	butter or margarine, cold
2 tbsp	30 mL	ice water

Chef's Tip

You can buy ready-to-bake pastry if you don't have time to make your own.

Directions for the Pastry:

1. Put the flour and butter in a mixing bowl. Using two butter knives or a dough blender, cut the butter into very small pieces until the mixture looks like crumbly oats.

2. Add the ice water and press the dough into a ball shape with your hands. Allow the pastry to sit for half an hour in the fridge.

Chef's Tip

Your hands may get sticky. Dusting your hands lightly with flour will help.

Rhubarb Filling

3 cups	750 mL	fresh or frozen rhubarb, chopped into 1/2-inch (1.25-cm) pieces
4 tbsp	60 mL	white or brown sugar
1 tbsp	15 mL	all-purpose flour
1/2 tsp	2.5 mL	cinnamon
1 tbsp	15 mL	butter, cut into pieces

Directions for the Tart:

1. Preheat oven to 375°F (190°C).

2. Place the chopped rhubarb in a large mixing bowl. Add the sugar, flour, and cinnamon and give the mixture a stir. Set aside.

3. Clean your work surface and sprinkle a tablespoon of flour directly on it. Gently roll out your pastry ball, flipping it over to stop it from sticking to the rolling pin and counter. The pastry should be thin (1/4 inch) and large enough to hold the rhubarb and allow the outer edges to be folded up.

4. Carefully place the pastry on a baking sheet lined with parchment paper. Transfer the rhubarb to the middle of the pastry. Arrange the chopped butter on top of the rhubarb. Fold the outer edges of the pastry up, to partly cover the rhubarb.

5. Place the tart in the oven to bake for 45 minutes, or until the pastry is golden and the rhubarb filling has bubbled.

6. Once cool enough, cut into pieces and serve.

Chef's Tip

Try mixing it up! Apples and fresh or frozen berries are delicious with rhubarb.

Birthday Party

Enchanted Birthday Cupcakes with
Flower Petals, Berries and Fairy Dust

The seasons are gone, baking is the best.
At last, there's one special day unlike the rest.
It's Loli's birthday, surely to be fun.
All of her friends have gathered one by one.
Together they laugh and dream of fairies,
Knee deep in bowls of batter and berries.
The table is set with teacups and plates.
Unicorns and teddies patiently wait.
Spoonfuls of love and cupfuls of flour,
Magic sprinkles and cupcakes in the hour.
Flowers and ribbons of colour and such,
Loli adorns them with her clever touch.
With a happy heart, her song fills the air.
The greatest cupcakes are ones that are shared.

Enchanted Birthday Cupcakes with
Flower Petals, Berries and Fairy Dust

Enchanted Birthday Cupcakes

Makes 8 cupcakes

1 cup	250 mL	all-purpose flour (or 1/2 all-purpose and 1/2 whole wheat flour)
1/2 tsp	2.5 mL	baking powder
1/2 tsp	2.5 mL	baking soda
1/4 cup	60 mL	unsalted butter or margarine, softened
2/3 cup	165 mL	white sugar
1/2 tsp	2.5 mL	vanilla extract
1	1	large egg
1/2 cup	125 mL	buttermilk or milk
1 cup	250 mL	fresh or frozen berries (raspberries, blueberries, strawberries)

Chef's Tip

You can test your muffins by poking the middle with a toothpick. If it comes out clean, the muffins are done.

Directions:

1. Preheat oven to 400°F (200°C), with the oven rack in the middle.

2. In a large mixing bowl, whisk together the flour, baking powder, and baking soda.

3. In a separate bowl, beat the butter and sugar until fluffy. Add the vanilla and egg, and beat well.

4. In 3 batches, add the flour mixture to the butter mixture, alternating with buttermilk. Mix until combined.

5. Place paper muffin cups in a muffin tin. Spoon the batter evenly into the muffin cups. Scatter berries over top.

6. Bake until golden, 15–20 minutes. Allow cupcakes to cool before icing.

Magical Buttercream Icing

¼ cup	60 mL	butter or margarine, at room temperature
1 cup	250 mL	confectioner's (icing) sugar
1 tsp	5 mL	milk

Chef's Tip

Make the icing more magical by adding natural food colour such as beet juice or blue-berry purée.

Directions:

1. Cream the softened butter until fluffy. Add the sugar slowly while continuing to beat the mixture.

2. Add the milk, mixing for another 30 seconds until combined.

3. Pipe the icing onto the cupcakes and refrigerate until serving time.

4. Before serving, add your own special touch! Flower petals! Berries! Sprinkles! Magic!

Add your own family favourite recipe

Draw and colour your favourite food

CPSIA information can be obtained
at www.ICGtesting.com
Printed in the USA
BVHW022353231121
622402BV00001B/3